BYGONE SALE
and Ashton-on-Mersey

BY

Cliff Hayes

BEAVER
PUBLISHING

BEAVER PUBLISHING LIMITED

Published by Beaver Publishing Limited
in association with
Northern Publishing Services
28 Bedford Road
Firswood
Manchester
M16 0JA
Tel: 0161 862 9399

ISBN:1-85962-060-4

written by

Cliff Hayes

Printed by M.F.P. Design & Print
Longford Trading Estate
Thomas Street
Stretford
Manchester
M32 0JT
Tel: 0161 864 4540
Fax: 0161 866 9866

Further copies of this book can be obtained from
Saga Books
4 Town Square
Sale
M33 7WZ

ACKNOWLEDGMENTS: Thanks to Bill Newton for his help and the loan of some of the images, and to Jim Stanhope-Brown for his images. Thanks to Ted Grey for his help with the tram photographs, and to Pauline Wride for help with the Ashton-on-Mersey photographs. Thanks also to the staff of the Local History Library in Sale, both front and back cover pictures come from their collection.

Cover Photograph: School Road, just before the First World War. On the right is the property built by Samuel Brooks with Brooks' Bank on the corner. On the left you can just see the gates of the Wesleyan Chapel that was demolished in the late 1960's.

Back Cover: School Road, 1897, near the junction with Washway Road. The Bulls Head Hotel is on the right and you can see over to Ashton Lane.

SALE LOCAL HISTORY SOCIETY

Further details can be obtained from the Local History Library above Sale Library, (behind the Town Hall). This is also the ideal place to start if you want to find out more about your local area. They keep a large collection of books, leaflets and maps on the area and have a friendly and helpful staff. Finding out more about local history couldn't be easier. Go along to the Local History Library, above the Sale Library, behind the Town Hall.

INTRODUCTION

Sale itself, though it has a long history, was not of any great importance until the late 1700's when the Duke of Bridgewater brought his canal through the area. True, it was a crossing point on the River Mersey, and all river crossing points had some importance, but it was the northern side of the river at Stretford where most of the activity took place, indeed Streta (Roman for road) and ford (where you cross a river) made up the name Stretford. Sale was just a sparse ribbon development along this Roman road, the name coming from the salix (willow) that grew by the river edge. Ashton, the village where the ash trees grow, is a far older settlement. The first church south of the Mersey was at Ashton and the Lords of the Manor were far more concerned about the village of Ashton than what happened off the main road in what was no more than scrubland and peaty moorland that made up the area known as Sale.

Sale extended from the Mersey in the north to the Pelican Brook (pelican being a corruption of an olde English word, not the bird). Barrow Brook ran through the north of the area, and Baguley Brook ran into it. As the main road runs almost north to south it has been taken for many years that Sale is to the right of Cross Street and Ashton is to the left. It was the Bridgewater Canal in the 1770's that brought the first rush of work and men into the area. For the first time Sale Moor was looked upon to cultivate the garden produce that could easily be sent into Manchester along this new water-highway. This activity led to the Sale Moor Enclosure Act which received Royal Assent on April 5th, 1805.

When the railways came along, opening July 21st 1849 Manchester to Altrincham, the fate of Sale, as a suburban development was sealed. People were attracted to the area, and roads and houses started to be built. Luckily at about the same time the camera arrived, and here we present what that invention has recorded in Sale and Ashton over the last one hundred years.

Journeying from Manchester into Wales and to the important city of Chester took the traveller over the River Mersey at Sale, after you had paid the toll fee at Crossford Bridge. The Washway Turnpike Act was passed in 1765 and this Toll House was built shortly after. The charges ceased and the road became free in 1885. Crossford Bridge received its name from the ancient cross said to have stood on the Sale side of the River Mersey.

Washway Road, probably about the time of the First World War as a double decker tram heads back to Manchester from Altrincham disturbing the otherwise rural scene.

Sale and Ashton as they were a century ago.

Cross Street is not a very long street and takes its name from an old stone cross which stood at the ford of the River Mersey. It would have been where the front car park for T.G.I. Friday's is today. Normally, you would have expected this name to have changed over the years to say Cross Road or Crossway, but even though a lot of names did change in the Sale area the name of Cross Street never did, and today it is a busy dual carriageway rushing south to the charms of Cheshire or grinding north to work in Manchester.

This photograph from around 1905 is taken from the School Road/Ashton Lane junction, looking north on the A56. The man in white to the left of the picture is Mr Hampson standing outside his grocery shop, with the local postman in the road next to the Hovis delivery cart.

Below: Cross Street stops at the Bulls Head and here is a postcard from about 1908 with the photographer standing in Washway Road looking back down Cross Street. The open-topped tram, the Bull's Head in its original condition with its elaborate topping, the posed children and the policeman on point duty makes a charming picture.

Above: Cross Street, Ashton-on-Mersey, around 1910 looking towards Manchester. As Ashton-on-Mersey was to the left of Cross Street and Sale was to the right I suppose this picture could be labelled either Sale or Ashton-on-Mersey.

A view of Cross Street, Sale, about 1910 from the Edwardian Series of the local Grenville Company. This is one of those postcards that have travelled. It was posted on May 24th 1927 in Sale by James W. McGhee. James was either an Australian who was residing at 7 Sylvan Avenue, Sale, or he had been to Australia and specifically to Sale in Victoria, Australia, because he posted the card to Mayor Stevens of that far town saying how much alike the two towns were, and how this view looked very much like he remembered the Australian Sale. The post office delivered the card to Australia, but how did it get back to a Postcard Fair in Manchester?

Cross Street around 1920. You can place this picture easily if you look to the right where you can see the old cottages which were cleared for road widening. You can just make out part of the Post Office sign on the very left of the picture. Even in the middle of the last century when this major north/south route started to develop it was a wide thoroughfare. The original caption of this picture read Cross Street, Ashton-on-Mersey, which technically most of this picture is. When they built the present Post Office it was planned for the Sale side of the road. Ashton-on-Mersey Councillors complained of the danger that their electorate would have to face crossing the main road, so it was moved to its present site. I wonder why no one from Sale put forward the same argument, or could they cross the road faster?

The Wagon & Horses Hotel on Cross Street, Sale, was built in 1740 to provide rest and a change of horses for travellers on this important route. It was enlarged to the size we see in these pictures in about 1850. To the left: a photographer's delight, a wagon and horses passing the Wagon & Horses, which made a charming 1908 postcard. Below: we see the celebration held in 1902 at the end of the South African wars, when local people gathered outside the hotel to see the carcass of an ox paraded around Sale, and then roasted outside the hotel, and everyone given a piece.

The corner of Cross Street and School Road, Sale about 1950. Taken from an unposted card from a local firm that produced views of Sale after the War and ceased in the 1970's. Trying to date photographs from cars and advertisements can be quite tricky. One sight you do not often see today is a cyclist waiting for the traffic lights to change to green. The building just caught on the right is the Bull's Head, (Hardy's Ales) and all the shops on the left disappeared when the new Trafford Magistrates Court were built.

H. D. Walker's Garage on the corner of Cross Street and Glebelands Road, petrol was 1/3d per gallon in the early 1920's when the photograph was taken.

The whole of the area taking in Cross Street, Crossford Bridge, and the Stretford and Sale Ees, were in times past notorious for flooding. The word ''ees'' means an area which floods often and easily. Here in about 1909 we see traffic negotiating a watery Cross Street.

The Odeon Sale, with Ashbrooks the Furnishers next door. The cinema started life as the Pyramid Cinema on Monday, February 26th 1934 and there were a lot of 'Egyptian' features incorporated in the building. On opening night all the staff were dressed in appropriate costumes, with the manager as a Pharaoh, and the usherettes as slaves! It had cost £70,000 to build, and could seat 2,000 people, as well as including a first flour cafe. The Rank Organisation bought it in 1941 when it became the Odeon until it closed down in October 1981. It had a brief spell as the Tatton Cinema before giving way to video and modern technology in 1984 when it was converted into a night club.

Below: Cross Street, Sale at the start of the 1960's. Belisha Beacons and other street furniture had started to appear, but no sign yet of the dreaded yellow lines.

Looking across the Cross Street, Washway junction, into School Road, about 1920. The Bull's Head, built about 1879 still has its ornate top including the terracotta bulls heads. A policeman on traffic directing duty looks for some traffic to direct.

Two pictures of the same view over 25 years apart. Top is the older picture from the late 1940's, just after the War. The tram lines have gone, but the ornate posts which carried the power still wait to be taken away. The picture below includes a Ford Anglia and a Mini, and as the Odeon is still open it is probably around 1970.

A very early photograph showing the start of the 'Washway,' said to be named after the special construction of the road, to wash away, to the side, all surface water. No tram lines, but there are gas lamps along the road, so this picture is from around 1900.

Above: The swinging sixties in Sale, taken from a spot opposite what was then the Sale Locarno Ballroom. This building had been opened as the Sale Lido in 1935 with a 130ft swimming pool which was covered and used as a dance floor in the winter.

Looking down Washway Road from the School Lane, Cross Street Junction on an Edwardian postcard. This was a favourite view for photographers and postcard suppliers of the past, and compare this picture with those on pages 12 and 16. No sign, you will notice, of the Pyramid Cinema (Odeon Cinema).

Washway Road, but this is the Brooklands or southern end of it. A postcard from just before the Second World War.

Looking towards the junction of Washway and Marsland Road just after the 1939/1945 War. Things were tight and rationing was still in place, but you could always depend on the Manchester & Salford Equitable Co-operative Shop, seen here on the right. Do you remember your mother's 'divi' number? They do say that the 'divi' is coming back, well done the Co-op!

The Lodge at the start of The Avenue, which was laid out by John Brooks. The Avenue was the most sought after place to have your abode, no one was to be sold a plot unless they had money in the bank. Propective buyers had to attend church and be good living family men. Four years later, there was just Mr Brooks and one Sam Kilvert (Kilverts Lard) living there! John Brooks sold land to the Manchester South Junction and Altrincham Railway Company and part of the deal was that the station they built was to be called Brooklands Station.

The Pelican Hotel, Manchester Road c. 1900. Though technically the Pelican Hotel is in Altrincham, the boundary being the brook which passes underneath the road just where the tram is in this picture.

The brook which is Baguley Brook and Fairywell Brook combined, once had the name pell-e-kani in Saxon times, and it is a corruption of this name which led to the name of this well known hotel. The Pelican hotel in this picture was pulled down in 1933 for road widening and the present hotel rebuilt further back. Note the horse drawn coaches outside.

St. John's Church, Brooklands. The church still stands today on Brooklands Road but is shown in fine form on this postcard from the mid-1930's.

The caption on the original postcard states Northenden Road and Broad Road in Sale. This view has altered a lot since this postcard was issued in about 1912. The photographer was actually stood in what was the entrance to Sale Railway Station, and where the gentlemen are stood on the left, is Broad Road. Jones & Jackson, The Painters and Decorators, which stands in the middle of the picture, was soon to be bought out and replaced by a white-tiled building that is still there today. The horse and Hansom cab is obviously waiting for a fare from the railway station, and the dominating spire is of the Congregational Church that used to stand on Northenden Road.

Sale Bridge, the end of School Road looking over into Northenden Road. This postcard is just 200 yards back from the photograph on the previous page. You can still make out the Decorators on the corner and the Bridgewater Coal Depot that stood on the corner of Britannia Road. Note that the tram lines finished abruptly here, and the entrance to the Gentleman's Underground Toilets on the left.

Right: Looking down Broad Road, Sale c. 1965 and the white building on the right has taken the place of the Painters and Decorators, it was Quirk's Plumbers at the time of this picture. You can see the chimney of the boilers of Sale Swimming Baths on the right.

24

The Northenden Road and Marsland Road junction roughly a century ago. The building pictured on the left started as J. Woods General Store, and was for a time the offices of Elite Coaches, Sale, before they moved over to Conway Road. Could that be one of Elite's early coaches, with Tony feeding the horse?

Below: Northenden Road, Sale Moor c. 1908. Looking the other way from the picture above. The Legh Arms can be seen at the bottom of the street. Temple Road was to the left and Warrener Street to the right. There was a cinema on the corner of Temple Road for many years.

Above: The Northenden Road and Marsland Road junction taken about 1919. A tram waits at the end of the line ready to return to Piccadilly, Manchester. This of course is now part of the one-way system and roundabout at that junction.

Northenden Road, Sale c. 1919. A Procession of Witness from St. Anne's Church, Northenden Road, built in 1856. The children's bonnets and ladies decorated hats echo the relief at the end of the Great War.

Below: A charming scene on School Road from around the turn of the century.

School Road, Sale and a very early photograph from before the turn of the century. The shops in this row include Thomas Dodd the Grocer, Thomas Barlow, Watchmaker, and Jones's the Newspaper shop.

Below: A wintery scene of School Road, Sale, tacken in 1912

A view of School Road, during the Edwardian era. The cobbles road must have been uncomfortable for the lady on her bicycle in the days before Tarmacadam. The building on the right, proudly boasted that it was Boots Cash Chemist.

School Road, Sale, from around 1900. Tatton Road can be seen going off to the right. The building that dominates the picture is still there, and is still a Bank.

A postcard looking right down School Road, Sale, from end to end. It is hard to realise that the road running across the front of the picture is actually Cross Street to the left and Washway Road to the right, with the Bull's Head on the left and the premises of J. Clarke, a Tea Dealer nearer the camera.

Below: The New Palace Theatre was in Ashton Lane and when this photograph was taken in about 1950 '' Irish Eyes Are Smiling'' was showing with a matinee that very afternoon.

Ashton Lane was the continuation of School Road and here we see that lane in about 1903. Our Coffee & Tea Merchant, J. Clarke, is still there on the right. All these buildings were cleared away in the building of the new Trafford Magistrates Court.

St. Paul's Church, Sale. Started in 1882, the foundation stone was laid on July 15th, a Saturday, by Mrs Cunliffe Brooks. It was opened on June 30th 1883.

Dr. White

Sale Priory in 1922. Built about 1711 the Priory stood on Dane Road. The name seems to have been just given to the building, it was never actually a Priory, nor indeed is there any evidence to suggest that there was any religious connection. The nearest this building came to any sort of fame was when Dr. Charles White (inset) lived there, and it was at this time when the famous Sale Mummy (Hannah Beswick) was reportedly kept on the roof of this building. Dr. White died in 1813, but we still have Dr. White's Bridge crossing the Bridgewater Canal, and after the house was pulled down in 1932, the site became known as Priory Gardens.

34

It is thought that the first Sale Hall was built in 1600 and at the time the owner was Richard Massey. When the Hall was bought by Mrs Mary Worthington in around 1839 it was said to have been in such a poor state that it could not be saved and had to be pulled down and a new hall built. A stone on the front of the building had engraved in it J.M. 1600, M.W. 1840 M.W. is Mary Worthington, and 1840 was when the second hall was built, but J.M. stands for James Massey who came into his inheritance when he was 10 years old in 1603 after his father James died. Either they got it wrong in 1840 or the house was intended for the son and they had documents to show the original date of the building, which since 1840 have gone missing. The Hall, which was the home of the Massey family, stood on the lower side of Rifle Road, until 1920 when it was demolished.

A very rare view showing the inside of Sale Hall, on Rifle Road, around 1910. The drawing room is a wonderful absolute clutter, with photographs fighting for space on top of the grand piano, and oil paintings and portraits almost hiding the walls of the room. The Massey family home was demolished in 1920.

Of Sale Old Hall there is nothing now remaining. Shown here is the only connection, the 'Dove Cote' which luckily still survives, stuck away on the roundabout at the M63 junction for Sale Water Park.
(Picture W. Schofield).

Sale Park, Sale, says the caption on this 1912 postcard. Today it is better known as Worthington Park, and here we see the entrance at Cheltenham Drive. The Park has a memorial plinth to James Prescott Joule (inset), who died in Sale in 1889. The memorial was unveiled by Sir William H. Bailey in 1905. There was also a stone lion in the Park, which gave years of amusement to local children until the vandals started destroying it in the 1970's. It has since been moved into the Children's Library in Sale where it can still be seen today.

Another view of the entrance to Sale Park. This picture is earlier than the previous one, and was postmarked 2nd August 1904. Like many other Parks it was noted for its fine Bandstand and in the 1940's and 50's local children would spend many a pleasant afternoon watching the budgies and cockatiels in the large aviary. In the 1960's there were tennis courts in the area on the right of the picture.

Sale Grammar School for Girls, formerly the High School for Girls, Sale, which had begun as a Private School, pictured here in about 1960. Today it is a mixed Co-Educational Grammar School, as Trafford, which this school comes under is one of the few authorities to retain Grammar Schools.

A photograph from a century ago showing what we know as Jackson's Boat. Originally the inn was called the Bridge Inn and there was a ferry known as Jackson's Ferry after the family who owned it. They also owned and ran the Bridge Inn. When the ferry across the River Mersey was discontinued, and a footbridge built, (see right) it became known as Jackson's Bridge. The redundant ferry boat was kept outside the inn for many years, and this led to the name Jackson's Boat Inn. We do know that it is 20 yards over the boundary and inside Manchester but it is on the south side of the River and you do have to approach from Sale, unless on foot.

Text within the image:
ASHTON LANE.
NORTHENDEN ROAD
TOWN HALL.
SALE
THE LIDO AND WASHWAY ROAD

A composite card showing the pride of Sale c. 1948.

Below the oldest building left standing in Sale, the old cottage at 120 Cross Street. Built around 1650 and now nicknamed 'eyebrow cottage' this was once originally two dwellings and has seen many uses over the years.

A combination card of Brooklands on a Valentine Postcard from 1950. One of a wonderful series that the firm produced for many years.

Ashton-on-Mersey was very proud of its Civic Fountain which stood at the junction of Moss Lane and Ashton Lane. Above we see a photograph from around 1910 showing the fountain with its ornamental top and incorporating a post box. On the right we see the fountain in the early 1960's and although it has lost some of the height and features, it was, with the help of the bollards, still standing at the centre of the Moss Lane and Ashton Lane junction.

Below: Park Road, Ashton-on-Mersey around 1950. Our picture is looking down from Glebelands Road, with Bromley's shop on the left.

Top: A postcard from very early this century, captioned: 'Old Village, Ashton-on-Mersey'. What it is really showing is the top end of Green Lane, with the Buck Hotel, corner of Buck Lane, on the left. The wall nearest us on the left had the bowling green behind it. Shops on the right included Samuel Bonds, Grocery and Bakers.

Below: Church Lane, Ashton-on-Mersey c. late 1940's, looking down towards St. Martin's Church. The houses on Church Lane to the right are still there, but those on the left were cleared to build Towns Croft Lodge, Sheltered Homes, which opened in 1982.

Buck Lane, Ashton-on-Mersey around 1937, looking towards Green Lane and Church Lane.

The oldest cottages in Ashton-on-Mersey says the caption on this photograph from around 1900. Sadly they have not survived. This Cottage still had a hard earth floor when demolished in the early 1970's.

Harboro Road, Ashton-on-Mersey, around 1910. The original village of Ashton on Mersey pre-dates Romans and it was the lure of the countryside and selectiveness of the area that prompted developers to build their better class houses there. It was always going to be above the other developments that were taking place around railway stations and tram lines, giving easy access into the city.

A 1930's advertisement for houses.

Within the composite card:
ON LANE, SALE
CHURCH LA
ST. MARTIN'S CHURCH
ASHTON-ON-MERSEY

A composite card showing the highlights of the village of Ashton-on-Mersey from around 1950. The card shows four of the main streets of Ashton-on-Mersey, but I do not know if you have noticed, there is not one car on any of the pictures. The church of St. Martin's, started building c. 1300, with its old clock tower taking centre place on the post card.